Thomas St. Collier

A History of the Statue Erected to Commemorate the Heroic Achievement

of Maj. John Mason and His Comrades

Thomas St. Collier

A History of the Statue Erected to Commemorate the Heroic Achievement
of Maj. John Mason and His Comrades

ISBN/EAN: 9783337192143

Printed in Europe, USA, Canada, Australia, Japan

Cover: Foto ©ninafisch / pixelio.de

More available books at **www.hansebooks.com**

Thomas St. Collier

A History of the Statue Erected to Commemorate the Heroic Achievement
of Maj. John Mason and His Comrades

ISBN/EAN: 9783337192143

Printed in Europe, USA, Canada, Australia, Japan

Cover: Foto ©ninafisch / pixelio.de

More available books at **www.hansebooks.com**

A HISTORY

OF THE STATUE ERECTED

To Commemorate the Heroic Achievement

OF

MAJ. JOHN MASON

AND HIS COMRADES,

WITH

An Account of the Unveiling Ceremonies.

— — —

COMPILED BY

THOMAS S. COLLIER.

SECRETARY OF THE NEW-LONDON COUNTY HISTORICAL SOCIETY

————◆————

PUBLISHED
BY THE COMMISSION.
1889.

CONTENTS.

———————— ..

THE MAJ. JOHN MASON STATUE.

THE BEGINNING OF THE STATUE.

The story of national and state testimonials of historic import, how they came to be thought of, and by what process of action and argument they were evolved, is always interesting, and deserves perpetuation in some lasting form; for usually such memorials are incentives to patriotism, and this is a feeling the nation and state should cultivate by all the means at their command.

In regard to the statue lately erected to the memory of Maj. John Mason and his comrades, on Pequot Hill, in the village of Mystic River, and town of Groton, Conn., this is particularly true. It is the memorial of a most heroic action, — an action that admitted of no delay, and which was carried out with a promptness, energy, and thoroughness that were the salvation of those colonists who had made New England their home.

The menace of war had changed to its actuality. Two hundred and fifty fighting men of all ages were called on to confront a nation numbering in its fighting men more than one thousand of the most cruel, daring, and courageous warriors of the red race.

Several men, women, and children of the inhabitants of Wethersfield and Saybrook had already experienced the nobility and
kindness of the Pequot heart, and their ashes were stirred and
scattered by each wind that swept past their torture-posts.

The people assembled in council, and ninety men volunteered to
march against the foe. John Mason, a soldier who had served in
the Netherlands, — that great school of war where William and
Maurice of Nassau, Sir Francis Vere, Lord Fairfax, Sir Philip
Sidney, Don John, Alva, Alexander Farnese, and Spinola, battled
and marched, — was selected to command these men, and in
May, 1637, set sail down the Connecticut River, and, taught by
the experience of his previous campaigning, skirted the shore
of the Sound until he had gained the rear of his enemy. There
he landed, and began his march through a country whose inhabitants would, at the first appearance of disaster to his force,
become enemies.

But, undaunted by the discouraging environments, he kept on,
his force reduced, by the necessity of leaving thirteen of his
people in the small craft that had brought him to the Narragansett shore, to seventy men.

Before him were the wilderness and a wily and courageous foe
numbering more than ten times his force; around him, a large
gathering of red men, whose deceitfulness was too well known to
admit of trust in their assertions; behind him, a settlement in
the wilderness, over whose scattered homes the shadow of sudden
and cruel death lay dark and gloomy.

To him and his seventy men the assembled colonists had committed the safety of themselves, their wives, and children. It was
their duty to be firm and brave in the trust, no matter what fate
lay before them; and with unfaltering step, and a heroism that
touched the sublime, they marched on, and fought, and conquered.

The colony was saved. Mason and his seventy men had met and overthrown the nation whose warriors had never before known defeat; had met them when they were entrenched in their stronghold, and had vanquished them both in desperate fight and in that cunning and strategy of which they were so proud. The homes and families of the colonists were saved; and, thanked by the Assembly whose orders he had so promptly executed, and honored by the entire community, Mason resigned his position as commander of the expedition, to be immediately appointed commander of the military forces of the colony, with the rank of major, a position that he held during the remainder of his life. His comrades were the heroes of the colony; and whenever occasion presented to do them honor, their neighbors gladly testified their respect and confidence by conferring office and trust to their care.

From this action followed a long peace, in which the colony thrived, and from which our present magnitude grew, and mankind derived the immense benefit that has resulted in the change of this continent from savagery to civilization.

It is a curious fact in our history that an event so pregnant with results, so heroic in execution, and so beneficial to the colonists, both of Connecticut and New England, should so long have remained without a memorial. But the agitation came; students of history proclaimed the fact that this was no unimportant affair, but one replete with significance : and public thought was turned to it.

The first article bringing the matter forward, that can be traced to its fountain-head, was that written by Mr. Amos A. Fish, published in the "Mystic Press," who sought to locate the site of the destroyed fort, and narrated such testimony to its location as was then existing in the neighborhood. This paper called forth many comments, among them a suggestion, emanating from the Rev.

Frederick Denison, that the site should be marked by a bowlder monument. A little later, Mr. Horace Clift, of Mystic River, published an account of the traditions of his family, the owners of the land, as to the location of the fort. These traditions, running through three or more generations, elicited the warm support of the Hon. William H. Potter, of Mystic River, who wrote a lengthy account of them, and brought the matter before the attention of the New-London County Historical Society, then presided over by the Hon. Lafayette S. Foster, of Norwich. The society took immediate interest in the matter, and appointed a committee of its members, consisting of the Hon. Richard A. Wheeler, of Stonington, Hon. William H. Potter, of Mystic River, and Daniel Lee, Esq., of New London, to locate the site of the fort, and prepare such reports as were necessary. These gentlemen called in to their assistance such residents of the neighborhood as had made the matter subject of study, among them Col. Amos Clift, the owner of the land. The site was located by the charred remains of the stockade, which still exist; and this done, the necessity of a monument to mark the spot was discussed, and agreed to; and Capt. William Clift, President of the Mystic-river Bank, deposited in that institution one hundred and fifty dollars, subject to the order of a monument committee. Drawings were prepared; but, owing to the excitement consequent on the beginning of our long array of national centennials, the matter lagged, though Messrs. Daniel Lee and William H. Potter made strenuous efforts to have something done during the lifetime of the memorial's projectors, and Capt. Elihu Spicer made a generous offer to furnish a sum sufficient for the purpose.

There was a divergence of opinion as to the design, however, and several were suggested, prominent among them being a combined representation of the Indian and white races. This difference led to delay, and one by one those who had interested themselves in the matter joined the silent majority, Hon. L. F. S. Foster, Hon. Henry P. Haven, Hon. W. H. Starr, and Messrs. Daniel Lee and Charles Allyn being of the number outside of Mystic, and in that village, Mr. A. A. Fish, Mr. Nathan Noyes, Col. Amos Clift, and others.

This brought the matter to a further stand; but in 1886 the New-London County Historical Society appointed a committee to bring the matter before the Legislature at its 1887 session, and the people of Mystic gave their aid. This committee consisted of Messrs. Richard A. Wheeler and William H. Potter, and it was associated with Messrs. Horace Clift, George W. Tingley, and others from the immediate vicinity of the fort's location. The committee appeared before the Legislature, at its 1887 session, and, though it met with much opposition, at last overcame all obstacles, and obtained an appropriation, the Legislature passing the following resolution : —

"Resolution concerning the erection of a monument to Captain John Mason.

"General Assembly, January Session, A.D. 1887.

"*Resolved by this Assembly:*

"SECTION 1. That three commissioners be appointed by the Governor to procure and cause to be placed on a bowlder monument, when such monument shall have been erected, on Mystic or Pequot Hill, in the town of Groton, Connecticut, a suitable bronze statue, of heroic size, of Captain John Mason.

"SEC. 2. Said commissioners are hereby authorized to make a contract, in the name and on behalf of the State, with some competent artist, to be by them selected, for constructing such statue and placing it in its position as aforesaid ; *provided*, that the whole expense of the statue and placing it in position shall be limited to a sum not exceeding four thousand dollars ; and *provided further*, that the amount so appropriated shall be paid out of the funds of the fiscal year of 1888."

Acting under the authority thus given, the Governor, Hon. P. C. Lounsbury, appointed Hon. Charles Augustus Williams, of New London, Charles E. Dyer, Esq., of Norwich, and Hon. Richard A. Wheeler, of Stonington. Mr. Williams was appointed chairman, and, at its first meeting, Thomas S. Collier, of New London, was elected the secretary of the Commission.

The New-London County Historical Society met, and appointed a committee, consisting of Messrs. Richard A. Wheeler, of Stonington, Oscar M. Barber, of Mystic Bridge, Henry Bill, of Norwich, W. H. H. Comstock, of New London, Rev. Charles J. Hill, of Stonington, Capt. John E. Williams and Horace Clift, of Mystic Bridge, and John J. Copp, of Groton, to solicit subscriptions and select a proper site for the monument; and those gentlemen quickly began work. Their solicitations were freely responded to, and they were soon able to proceed to business. The subscribers to the pedestal fund were —

William Clift	. $150 00
Elihu Spicer .	500 00
Elizabeth G. Stillman	100 00
C. H. Mallory .	50 00
Horace W. Fish .	50 00
C. A. Williams	25 00
Jeremiah Halsey .	20 00
Henry Bill .	20 00
William L. Palmer	10 00
Charles R. Stark	10 00

A total of nine hundred and thirty-five dollars.

With this sum, a bowlder, weighing twenty-three tons, was transported to the spot selected, and a die of cut granite was placed on it. The ground to place the statue in a striking position had been donated by Messrs. Horace and Edmund Clift; and the pedestal being completed, and a neat coping of granite placed around it, the committee reported to the Commission that the pedestal was ready for inspection.

The Commission then met at the site of the proposed monument, and, finding the pedestal a fine and notable structure, accepted the same, and began the work of obtaining a suitable statue to place thereon.

THE WORK OF THE COMMISSION.

THE pedestal for the monument to Maj. John Mason being complete, and accepted by the Commissioners appointed by the Governor of the state to procure a memorial to be placed thereon, they, at their next meeting, invited artists to send in competitive designs for an heroic bronze statue, suitable for this purpose. This was done by advertisement and letter, and the day appointed for selection was September 15, 1888. At that time, five models, and one photographic reproduction of a model, were brought to the rooms of the Commission, which failed to make selection, the meeting adjourning for one week.

Mr. Robert Kraus, who had submitted a design, withdrew from the competition before the adjourned date, and the competitors were J. Scott Hartley, of New York, Karl Gerhardt, of Hartford, H. K. Bush-Brown, of Paris, Alexander M. Calder, of Philadelphia, and J. G. C. Hamilton, of Westerly. After due examination and interchange of views, the model of Mr. Hamilton, submitted by the Smith Granite Company, of Westerly, R.I., was made choice of, and the Commission entered into a contract with that company and its sculptor, Mr. Hamilton, whereby the last-named parties agreed to furnish and place on the pedestal erected on Pequot Hill, Groton, an heroic bronze figure of a Puritan warrior, the statue to be in place by June 6, 1889.

During the work on the model, the Commissioners visited the studio of Mr. Hamilton, and gave their personal attention to the figure and costume. Mr. Hamilton's careful study had made suggestion useless, however, and when the model was completed, application for a sum sufficient to unveil the statue with appropriate ceremonies was made to the Legislature of 1889 and granted.

When assured of this, the Commission made the programme for that occasion its study, and the following scheme was adopted: A procession of civic and military bodies from the central part of the village to the site of the statue ; music ; prayer ; the delivery of the statue to the state ; its acceptance ; music ; oration ; poem ; music ; procession to the central part of the village ; dinner to military and invited guests.

It was decided to ask the Hon. John T. Wait to deliver the oration, and in case he could not officiate, Mr. Isaac H. Bromley was named as alternate. Mr. Wait was forced to decline, and Mr. Bromley accepted the position. The Rev. Charles J. Hill was invited to make the opening prayer ; the Rev. G. H. Miner was asked to offer the benediction, and Thomas S. Collier was selected as the poet. The chairman of the Commission was asked to take charge of the order of exercises, and to make the address delivering the statue to the state, which was to be accepted by the Governor, and the Rev. D. H. Miller, D.D., was invited to ask the blessing at the dinner.

These gentlemen having accepted the duties asked of them, the programme was satisfactorily arranged. The contractors reporting the statue ready for placing in position, the Commission set June 6, 1889, as the date when they could attend and see it so placed. Mr. C. A. Williams, chairman, being obliged to visit California on business of importance, the Commission voted that Mr. Charles E. Dyer should be chairman during his absence.

In compliance with their agreement with the Smith Granite

Company, the Commission visited Mystic River on June 6th, and saw the statue placed in position. They then met several gentlemen of the village, and with them made arrangements for the unveiling ceremonies, which were set for Wednesday, June 26, 1889.

Gen. Edward Harland, of Norwich, to whom the marshalship had been offered, having informed the Commission that it would be impossible for him to serve, Gen. Charles T. Stanton, of Stonington, was selected, and accepted.

The Commission then asked Capt. John E. Williams, Dr. Oscar M. Barber, and Horace Clift, Esq., all of Mystic Bridge and Mystic River, to act as a committee of entertainment, and assist the Commission. Col. W. W. Packer, Capt. J. Alden Rathbone, Capt. George E. Tripp, and Elias Williams, Esq., were requested to act as marshals and assist Gen. Stanton ; and E. Burrows Brown, Esq., A. H. Simmons, Esq., and Col. James F. Brown were asked to act as a reception committee. These gentlemen very kindly assented, and the ceremonies of unveiling, and the duties of the day were all cared for. The arrangements were completed, and the guests invited by Thursday, June 20.

Among the people invited were the Governor and his staff, and the state officers : the Governors and Lieutenant-Governors of Massachusetts and Rhode Island ; the Appropriation Committee of the Legislature ; the senators and representatives from the towns and districts contiguous to the place : representatives of the Massachusetts, Rhode Island, and Connecticut state historical societies; and from the New-England Historic Genealogical Society; the American Antiquarian Society, of Worcester ; the New-Haven Colony Historical Society ; the New-London County Historical Society ; and the Plymouth Museum and Library. Citizens of the state, and people interested in such matters, were generally invited, and the list of guests numbered one hundred and fifty.

The day of the unveiling was foggy, but not enough so to prevent a successful celebration. The guests, military and civic, reached Mystic by eleven A.M., and were quickly formed in column, and, headed by the Governor's Foot-Guards, proceeded to the site of the statue, where a platform and seats had been arranged. The procession began its march at 11.35 A.M., the time set in the programme being 11.30. The ceremonies at the statue began at 12.30 P.M., the hour set, and were concluded in time for the dinner to begin at the appointed time, 3.00 P.M.; and at 5.30 the guests were all in New London, the ceremonies having passed without break or hindrance.

Among the guests present and not before mentioned were the Hon. John T. Wait, of Norwich; Hon. Charles A. Russell, M. C., of Killingly; Hon. Charles Francis Adams, of Boston; Hon. Thomas R. Trowbridge, of New Haven; Hon. Benjamin Stark, of New London; John C. Wyman, Esq., of Valley Falls, R. I.; Elisha Turner, Esq., of Torrington; Rev. J. Gibson Johnson, D.D., of New London, and many gentlemen from Norwich, New London, Stonington, and the three villages of Mystic, Mystic River, and Mystic Bridge.

Many descendants of Maj. John Mason were also present, and shared in the hospitalities of the Commission; and the Hon Richard A. Wheeler, one of the Commissioners, carried Maj. Mason's sword on the platform.

The unveiling ceremonies were universally satisfactory, and the statue was as unanimously decided to be a fine and suitable representation of the man whose heroic deeds it commemorated.

The statue is a notable production, representing the typical Puritan of history,— a man ready of purpose, courageous in action, holding a firm faith in his mission as a propagator of the truth of God's Word, and of the divinely bestowed right of freedom.

The figure is about nine feet high, with a fine poise, denoting

strength and action, with the right hand grasping the half-drawn
sword. The costume is that of the colonists of the period, and
allows of freer scope in drapery than the stiff garments of the
present permit.

The pedestal consists of a panelled die, standing on a double
base, the upper cut, the lower a natural bowlder weighing more
than twenty-three tons. The total height of pedestal and statue
is about twenty feet.

The statue stands in a commanding position on the crest of
Pequot (or Mystic) Hill, at the junction of two roads, in a circle
curbed with granite. The Sound, with its islands, the villages of
Mystic River, Mystic Bridge, and Noank, the borough of Stonington, the picturesque valley of the Mystic, and the varied shore-line
of the Sound make the view an exceptionally fine one.

The battlefield lies a short distance north of the statue, but from
the fact that arrow-points are found thickly scattered all over the
level space and gradual slope contiguous to the site of the monument, it seems safe to infer that the fight raged even beyond the
site selected as best suited for placing the memorial.

The inscription on the base is :

ERECTED A.D., 1889,
BY THE STATE OF CONNECTICUT,
TO COMMEMORATE THE HEROIC ACHIEVEMENT OF
MAJOR JOHN MASON
AND HIS COMRADES, WHO NEAR THIS SPOT,
IN 1637, OVERTHREW THE PEQUOT INDIANS,
AND PRESERVED THE SETTLEMENTS FROM DESTRUCTION.

The statue is indeed a worthy memorial of a most heroic
action.

THE UNVEILING CEREMONIES.

THE visiting companies formed as directed by the marshals, and, headed by Gen. Charles T. Stanton, chief marshal, began the line of march at 11.35 a.m. The leading organization in line was the First Company of the Governor's Guards, commanded by Maj. Kinney, and headed by Colt's Band. The Guards escorted the Governor and his staff, riding in carriages.

They were followed by a battalion of four companies of the Third Regiment, Connecticut National Guard, and the Machine Gun platoon of the regiment, which were headed by the regimental band.

The Commission, orator, poet, state officers, members of the Legislature, and invited guests, filling twenty-seven carriages, formed the last division of the procession, and were headed by Tubbs's Band.

Arriving at the statue, the invited guests took seats on the platform, and at 12.30 the ceremonies were opened by the Third-Regiment Band playing " America."

Mr. Charles E. Dyer, the chairman of the Commission, then said : —

" It is eminently appropriate on this spot, around which cluster so many hallowed recollections, consecrated by the blood of our forefathers, connecting intimately the present with the past, and bringing to mind the watchful care of our Heavenly Father from the days of our colonial existence to the present hour, that the blessing of God should be invoked. I therefore call upon the Rev. Charles J. Hill, of Stonington, to open the exercises with prayer."

PRAYER.

Almighty and ever glorious God, we adore thee as the King of kings and Lord of lords, the Governor of the universe, and the Ruler of nations.

We recognize thy hand in the foundation of this nation. We acknowledge our belief that thou didst bring our fathers across the sea ; guide them through the wilderness ; deliver them from their enemies ; and lead them by a way they knew not unto the city of habitation.

One generation shall praise thy works to another, declare the might of thy terrible acts, and utter the memory of thy great goodness. Thou didst bring out fathers to the borders of this sanctuary, even to this mountain which thy right hand had purchased ; thou didst cast out the heathen before them, and divide them an inheritance by line, and make them to dwell in safety. Oh that men would praise the Lord for his goodness ! and for his wonderful works to the children of men !

O thou who hast been our dwelling-place in all generations ! grant that we may dedicate this monument and unveil this statue not for worship, not for sacrifice, not for human glory, but as a witness to this generation, and a testimony to our children's children of our faith in the God of our fathers, who saved them from destruction, and delivered them out of the hand of their enemies. O God ! we dedicate it to thee.

Let it be to all the people a memorial of thy faithfulness — a token of thy mercy — a pledge of thy help in every time of need. Let it be an acknowledgement of our gratitude to those who fought our battles, and saved our fathers from death and our mothers from suffering. May it teach us to be loyal to duty, brave in times of trouble, and heroic in saving those who are in danger!

O thou who art merciful! we confess that all our deeds are marred by ignorance and weakness, even when they are not defiled by sin : and we acknowledge with shame and confusion of face that we have not been faithful to the high trust thou didst commit to us, when thou didst send our fathers across the sea to teach the ignorant savages thy Gospel, and declare unto them the true character of the Great Spirit whom they ignorantly worshipped ; but hear, Thou in heaven, thy dwelling-place, and pardon, we beseech thee, the sins of the penitent people. We thank thee for a clearer conception of the Gospel of Salvation, and pray that its spirit, abiding in our hearts, may lead us to be kind to the weak, just to the unfortunate, merciful to the erring, and atone, by an enlarged Christian benevolence, for the wrongs that may have been done in the past. Let schools, and institutions of industry, and churches, reared by a penitent nation, be memorials of our obligations to " the children of the forest," into whose heritage we have entered. And so we pray thee, let the memory of the past inspire our gratitude and promote our love for one another. And may the time speedily come when the Gospel of Him who died for the redemption of the world shall fill the whole land with peace and good-will to men, and the hope of life everlasting!

And unto the Father, and unto the Son, and unto the Holy Ghost everlasting thanks shall be given. And let all the people say, Amen.

Mr. Dyer then made the following address, delivering the statue to his Excellency the Governor : —

" YOUR EXCELLENCY, — We are assembled to participate in exercises appropriate to the completion of a statue erected in memory of the heroic Maj. John Mason, who with his comrades, near this spot, won a signal victory over their savage foes a little more than two hundred and fifty years ago.   Pequot Hill is a locality that will be ever memorable.   Here it was that the decisive blow was struck by which the salvation of the infant colony was secured, and the settlements were preserved from annihilation.

" The commissioners to whom the responsibility was assigned to ' procure and cause to be placed on a bowlder monument, on Mystic (or Pequot) Hill, in the town of Groton, Connecticut, a suitable bronze statue of heroic size of Maj. John Mason,' have discharged the duty committed to their care.

" The structure is complete, and we now deliver it to you, sir, the honored chief magistrate and official representative of the state ; and may the God of nations, who guided and sustained him whose memory and whose deeds we seek this day to perpetuate in granite and in bronze, watch over and protect our beloved commonwealth and this united, happy, and prosperous nation, throughout the years to come ; and may we, the citizens thereof, relying on his unerring wisdom, be ever mindful of the motto emblazoned on the banner of our state, *Qui Transtulit Sustinet.*"

To this the Governor replied in the following words : —

" Memorials hastily erected to commemorate patriotic deeds or distinguished services are not always the best evidence of the gratitude of a nation or state, or unquestioned test of true merit.

The deeds and services which are intended to recall the history of a nation, written or unwritten, transmitted from one generation to another, recounting the unselfish devotion and self-sacificing, patriotic zeal of her children, are broader and higher ground from which to form a judgment of the men and scenes of the times in which they were participants. We have met here to-day, after a lapse of more than two centuries, to recall to our minds a man so prominently identified with the history of the little colony which developed into the broad and prosperous State of Connecticut, that his acts and daring deeds have survived these centuries and become part of the history of the state. A grateful people, through its government, directed this memorial statue to be erected here amid scenes of which Maj. John Mason was the leader and the daring spirit. The skilful hand of the designer has well displayed, in silent bronze, the brilliant, daring Indian fighter. Mr. President, on behalf of the state, I accept the charge of this monument, and extend hearty thanks for the fidelity with which the Commission has discharged its trust."

Music by Tubbs's Band followed, and Mr. Dyer then said : —

" LADIES AND GENTLEMEN. — It gives me pleasure to introduce to you, as the orator of this occasion, a native of New-London County, a man whom you all know, — Mr. Isaac H. Bromley, of Boston."

ORATION.

For fourteen years, beginning with the nineteenth of April, 1875, anniversary of the first bloodshed of the Revolution at Lexington, and ending last month with a fitting celebration of the inauguration of the first President of the Republic, we have been passing through a series of centennial observances. For all the great initial points in the nation's history, we have set up our century-posts, while around them we have ranged our memory-tents and built our solemn altars. The fourteen years between the shot fired by the embattled farmers — "heard round the world" — and the salvo of artillery that punctuated the inaugural oath of the first President, were filled with the travail pains which ended in the bringing forth of a man-child among the nations. We have just finished celebrating that birthday of fourteen years.

During this period, the minds of sixty million people have been occupied with memories of those whom they fondly call "the fathers"; with reverent admiration for their virtues, lofty appreciation of their sacrifices, and boundless gratitude for the priceless legacy they left to their descendants. It is doubtless true that, looking somewhat through the medium of our own emotions down the long perspective of a hundred years, we have magnified events that in their day seemed but ordinary, and glorified men who, to their contemporaries, were common mortals. But have we erred in this? Is the glamour which a hundred years have thrown over these events more misleading than the mists through which contemporaries viewed them? Is the halo with which we surround our heroes more unreal than the canvas of the artist who, with his sitter close at hand, only painted him skin deep?

If our judgments of the long-gone past and the actors in it are not characterized by the cold, hard accuracy of scientific statement, is it not also true that only in the historic perspective do we discern the true proportions of character and the real relations of events?

The fathers builded indeed better than they knew. Of the full meaning of their work, and of their own future fame as its authors, none of them had any adequate conception, and but few had dimly dreamed. Neither they nor their work could be fairly judged in their own time, for with all the success that had attended their endeavors, the fulfilment of their highest hopes in the establishment of the Union, it must be remembered that they saw but the beginning of an experiment. Only in the light of a hundred years of trial can the work of the fathers, and the fathers themselves, be fairly judged. Looking back across the years, we see their figures stand out, clear cut, massive, dominant, larger than human, on the sky-line of our history. We know now, what they did not, the vast results that trembled in the balance against their fortitude and faith; and in that knowledge we have said in the pride of our ancestry and the fervor of our gratitude, "All these were 'Plutarch's men.'" It is not we who have idealized them, but that silent, ceaseless process in the crucible of time that never fails to purge the characters of the men who greatly served their age of all the dross of human frailty, leaving only the pure gold of their lives for our admiration. Only our ideals are real. For that alone lives which we make live by remembering, and that only is dead which has been forgotten.

It so happens that, at the close of this series of centenary anniversaries of the formative period of the government, we are bidden by this occasion to take a more extended retrospect; to review some of the events, and to consider the character of another of "Plutarch's men," of a still earlier time. We shall see that largely through what happened on this hill two hundred and fifty-two years ago, and through the courage, skill, and promptitude in emergencies of the man whose memory we are here to honor, the whole succession of events we have so lately commemorated was made possible.

Just here upon this spot the tide was turned that, with gathering force, threatened to overwhelm the small beginnings of that New-England civilization which a hundred and fifty years later became the vital force of a new nation. And it was he whose memory we are honoring to-day who in the crisis of the fight gave the decisive word. Fearful word it was; it meant relentless fire and indiscriminate slaughter; but it said "Thus far, no farther," to the refluent waves of barbarism, and cleared the way to forty years of peace.

John Mason was born in England about 1601. Neither the place nor the date of his birth is precisely known, nor do we know anything definite of his family. Of the influence of local surroundings, hereditary tendencies, and early associations upon the development of his character, we are accordingly left almost entirely to conjecture. We may well suppose that he first saw the light in one of those counties in the North of England, — Lincoln, York, or Nottingham, — where such men as Robinson, Brewster, and Bradford were bred, and that his youth was influenced by the atmosphere of their pious teachings and austere lives. Or it may be that his first infant cry was heard somewhere on the banks of Severn, whose waters two hundred years before had prefigured the dissemination of Wyckliffe's doctrines when they bore his dust to the spreading sea. However that may be, we cannot be far wrong in assuming that his first breath was of an air vital with protest and dissent and strenuous assertion of individual freedom of thought, belief, and speech; that he inherited from a vigorous though obscure ancestry his sound mind and sinewy frame; that his training was strict and severe; and that his associations were with that common people of England who stood up for their own against the menaces of the Stuart kings in Parliament and Prince Rupert's fiery charge on Marston Moor.

The forward movement of the world in history is by cycles. To long intervals of rest and inaction succeed periods of stormy dispute, clashing of interests, social upheavals, political revolutions, tempests and tumults of war. To these convulsions succeed again the rest and rust of peace, too often paid for by intellectual stagnation, deadened patriotism, and moral degeneracy. It is not in the slothful contentment of these stagnant intervals that life is most worth living. They furnish little illumination for the pages of history, evoke no heroes or martyrs to elevate and ennoble the race by grand examples of courage and self-sacrifice.

In our own time, who that lived in and was part of the great contention that covered so many years of violent controversy and hot debate culminating in civil war, does not thank God that his lot was cast in such a stirring and eventful time? What good fortune it was to the contemporaries of Washington and Putnam and Green, of the signers of the Declaration and the authors of the Constitution, to have walked abreast of that procession of events in such grand company!

It was the good fortune of John Mason to enter on the stage of action, not in the piping times of peace when the king ruled undisputed, the peasant meekly bore his yoke, and the world was stagnant with content, but in a time that bristled with questionings and quivered in every fibre with the tokens of a new revelation and a new birth.

It was eighty years since Martin Luther had uttered his immortal answer: "Here stand I; I can none other; God help me. Amen." The protest had made little stir in the visible England which seemed so pliant to Wolsey, so submissive to the king. But though the momentary restlessness to which Wyckliffe had quickened the thought of England a hundred and fifty years before seemed to have utterly disappeared, he had not, as the result showed, scattered seed on barren ground. The immediate impulse which proceeded from him had indeed ceased, but for a hundred years thereafter manuscript copies of his translations and tracts were in circulation among the common people, who met in groups to hear them read, or passed them on from hand to hand. The foundation for protest lay very deep in English soil. When Henry, pressed by political necessities, entered the lists in defence of the Pope and against Luther, though he gained for himself the title of "Defender of the Faith," outside the narrow circle of his courtiers and dependents he was unheard and unheeded. But when, a little later, he made his stand against papal supremacy, and asserted for himself the Headship of the Church, the common people of England, in whom the teachings of Wyckliffe had been slowly taking root through two hundred years, smothering their indignation and disgust at the shameful motives of the king, and seeing only in the whole transaction the rescue of the English government and people from subjection to papal domination, gave him at once, and heartily, their sympathy and support.

But neither political nor religious freedom was to be established in the lust of a royal Bluebeard. The people had only changed masters. The struggle against absolutism was to go on for another hundred years, until a king's head lay upon the block; and the practice of religious toleration was to wait enforcement until, in a land then almost unknown, a colony of refugees from religious intolerance should drive out from among them, for a difference in belief, the founder of a state where " soul liberty" was first established.

The small gain secured to freedom of opinion by Henry's breach with the Pope seemed hopelessly lost in the bloody reign of Mary ; but Elizabeth's accession to the throne had revived the hopes of the persistent heretics who had outlived Mary's persecutions. Elizabeth's reign, so fruitful of results of tremendous import to England and to all mankind, was now, at John Mason's birth, within two years of its close. Never in the annals of the kingdom had there been such intellectual activity, such rapid growth and expansion of the mind and heart of the people as in the reign just ending. The issue raised by Luther was still under discussion, and the professed believers in a gospel of peace and good-will were burning, shooting, and torturing one another over the question which of the two parties into which Christendom was divided was the rightful representative of that gospel's author. England, though she had stood under arms on all her coasts at the approach of the Armada, had not felt the contact of actual war. But she had sent her soldiers over into the Netherlands to fight against Philip, and these had brought back on their return a zeal for the new religion quickened by their association with the Netherlanders, and a hatred of the papacy intensified by what they had witnessed of the cruelties of Alva.

It was only natural that the intellectual movement of the period should in these conditions revolve largely round religious themes. The book most circulated and read among the common people was the Bible, newly translated by Tyndale. With the unusual interest attaching to it from its having been so long forbidden. and the subject of so wide and fierce contention, we may well imagine the eager curiosity with which they fell upon the stirring recital of the trials and triumphs of the chosen people in the Old Testament, and the burning zeal with which they debated the doctrines of the New.

Nor was it strange that to these people, painfully working out
their own deliverance amid cruel persecutions and bloody wars,
the story of the chosen people, of their fierce and uncompromising
spirit, their merciless extermination of the enemies of Jehovah, and
the miraculous interferences by which they triumphed over their
foes, should have a special charm. For they, too, were a chosen
people, and there were not lacking seers among them in whose
bosoms throbbed the consciousness that their Passover was at
hand, and that for them also there waited the parted waters and
the promised land. They were of the Mosaic dispensation. It
was not the peaceful slope of Olivet that inspired their meditations
or occupied their view. It was Sinai that always stood over them,
black and gloomy with clouds, threatening with its thunders and
terrible with its swift lightnings. And we shall see them before
long, slaying their Amorites hip and thigh, smiting them with the
sword until none are left alive, and then possessing their land.

The great religious contention was at its height when John
Mason was born. Two years after Elizabeth's death, Grotius
wrote that theology ruled in England. It occupied the minds and
filled the thought of king and people to the exclusion of almost
everything else. A historian of the time writes: "Sunday after
Sunday, day after day, the crowds that gathered round the Bible
in the nave of St. Paul's, or the family group that hung on its
words in the devotional exercises at home, were leavened with a
new literature. Legend and annal, war-song and psalm, state-
roll and biography, the mighty voices of prophets, the parables of
evangelists, stories of mission journeys, of perils by the sea and
among the heathen, philosophic arguments, apocalyptic vision, —
all were flung broadcast over minds unoccupied for the most part
by any rival learning."

So much, in briefest outlines, of the intellectual environment in
which he first drew breath, and of the influences which shaped his

career. is necessary to a proper understanding of Mason's character and conduct.

Our first knowledge of him — and that but very scanty — is as a lieutenant under Sir Thomas Fairfax, serving in the Low Countries. How long he remained there we do not know. He could not have served long with Fairfax, as the latter's service, which was somewhat in the nature of a youthful adventure, was but for the few months of the siege of Bois-le-Duc, — from April to July, 1630. That he was of good extraction and a young man of promise is indicated by his rank of lieutenant. The fact that Sir Thomas Fairfax remembered him some fourteen or fifteen years later. and sent to him across the ocean an urgent request to return to England and accept a Major General's commission in the Parliamentary Army, is proof that under the eye of Sir Thomas he had demonstrated his courage and capacity. Lord Fairfax was, even at that age, a keen observer and a shrewd judge of men, and being himself one of the ablest and pluckiest soldiers of his age, he knew a soldier when he saw him.

If Mason was in the Low Countries with Fairfax in 1630, he could not have been in Warham's company, which arrived at Massachusetts in May of that year and presently fixed themselves at Mattapan, — afterwards called Dorchester. That he was among the earliest accessions to the Dorchester colony is apparent, however, from the fact of his appearing in December, 1632, as engaged under a commission from the governor and magistrates of Massachusetts to search for a pirate named Bull, who had for some time been harassing the settlers on the coast.

Two years later, he was one of a committee appointed to plan the fortifications of Boston harbor, and was presently in charge of the erection of a battery on Castle Island, from which it would appear that he had had some experience in engineering.

In March, 1635, he represented Dorchester at the General

Court.   Later in the same year, it is probable that he accompanied
the party of adventurers who made the difficult journey to the
banks of the Connecticut, opening the way for the larger emigration which, with Hooker and Stone, in June, 1636, settled at
Windsor.

It was not until after long and heated discussion — all discussion was hot in those days — and a close vote of the General
Court, that permission was granted for this emigration.   From
what happened later, from the character and subsequent career of
Hooker, and from the circumstance that the Connecticut emi-
grants, in the organization of their government, did not found the
civil franchise on church membership, it may be safely inferred
that a prime motive for this emigration was the desire to establish
a social system in which there should be an entire separation
between church and state.   The part taken in it by John Mason
discloses the bent of his mind in the direction of freedom of
conscience.

At Windsor, as everywhere else in New England where colonies
were established, the church pastor was the leader.   Hooker was
the prominent figure and chief factor in the early life of the
Windsor colony and of the state.   For it was almost purely
a religious movement that colonized New England : the colonists
were, in fact, religious exiles.   And if, in the clearer light of
to-day, the founders of New England seem to have been at times
fanatical, bigoted, and intolerant, let us remember with profound
gratitude that we are largely indebted to the rigor of discipline
and severity of training which these qualities engendered for the
pure stock and distinctive New-England character of which we
are so proud.   The half-breed races of Spanish America on one
side, and French Canada on the other, are illustrations of the
social conditions from which the rigid morality of the Puritan
delivered us.

The immediate neighborhood of the Mathers, and Brewsters, and Bradfords, could not have been especially attractive to persons of a cheerful temper or lively disposition. The steady diet of the psalm-singers was the wrath of God. To indulge in pleasantry under such a dispensation was unpardonable levity, to be visited with censure, and possibly with stripes. Doubtless the company of Morton and his fellow roysterers at Merry Mount had largely the advantage in point of liveliness and gayety. But these were two extremes, and there was no mean. They could not get on together. It was not quite in the spirit of what, in our day, is called liberty, but it was clearly a good day's work, when Miles Standish took Morton by the collar, faced him towards England, and broke up his hold. The psalm-singer stayed. It was well he did, for in that Puritan strain, which was simply the old Saxon at white heat with religious zeal, and hardened with the hammer of religious persecution, lay all that makes the nation great and prosperous.

The three settlements, Hartford, Windsor, and Wethersfield, which then constituted Connecticut, contained in 1636 about eight hundred persons. They were surrounded by tribes of savage Indians, estimated at from three thousand to four thousand, most of whom were unfriendly, some actively hostile. From their nearest civilized neighbors they were fourteen days distant, beyond the hope of any succor against sudden attack. From the Connecticut River to the Pawcatuck, the country was roamed over — the pseudo-philanthropist will observe the distinction between roaming over and occupying — by the Pequots and Mohegans; the country east of the Pawcatuck was claimed by the Narragansetts. Sassacus, chief of the Pequots, had under him twenty-six sachems, one of whom was Uncas, of the Mohegans. Jealousy between the latter and his chief had caused bad blood, so that Uncas was quite ready when the issue came to side with the whites against

Sassacus ; and questions of boundary had kept the Pequots and Narragansetts arrayed against each other. So it happened, or, as the colonists devoutly believed, was specially ordered by Providence, that Sassacus, in the war which soon broke out, was left without the aid of two natural allies, with either of whom he could have exterminated the white settlers of New England.

It is useless to deny that the whites had given good cause for the hostility of the aborigines. It was a real grievance, and not innate treachery and vindictiveness, that lay at the root of the whole business. It dated from Thomas Hunt's seizure and sale into slavery, in 1614, of twenty-four inoffensive Indians who had trusted in his honor. The vindictive feeling aroused by this brutal outrage, which had been somewhat allayed in the breast of Canonicus by the fair dealing of the Plymouth colonists, burned unquenched in the bosoms of Sassacus and the Pequots, who made no discrimination between the unprincipled adventurer of 1614 and the peaceably-disposed settlers of the later period.

In 1634, Captain Stone, a trader from Virginia, having put into Connecticut River in a small vessel, was killed with his whole crew by a party of Pequots. The demand of the Massachusetts authorities for the surrender of the murderers was met by Sassacus with excuses, prevarications, and delays, which continued through two years, when the killing of John Oldham, of Watertown, Mass., by a party of Pequots from Block Island, brought matters to an issue and war was formally declared.

It was not a war, however, that the Massachusetts colonists had any special cause to be proud of. An expedition was fitted out, consisting of ninety men, in three small vessels, under command of John Endicott, which, sailing away to Block Island, attacked the Indians there, killing some fourteen of them, burning their houses, cutting down their corn, and destroying their canoes. They then proceeded west to the mouth of the Pequot — now the

Thames — River, where they burned more houses and destroyed more crops, after which they returned to Boston. Capt. Lion Gardiner, in command of a garrison established at the mouth of the Connecticut, accurately described the expedition and its results, when he said: "You came hither to raise these wasps about my ears, and then you will take wings and fly away."

In the three towns of Wethersfield, Hartford, and Windsor were about two hundred and fifty white men capable of bearing arms. They were surrounded by Indian tribes, who, between the Hudson and Narragansett Bay could muster, if united, four or five thousand warriors. Of these, from seven hundred to one thousand were Pequots under Sassacus, now in open hostility. The wasps were raised and Endicott had sailed away.

The wily Sassacus made it his first endeavor to unite all the Indian tribes in a war of self-preservation, which meant extermination, against the colonists. To this end, he brought himself to send ambassadors to his ancient enemies, the Narragansetts, to induce them to come into the alliance. Meanwhile, the Pequots in scattered bands were harassing the Connecticut settlers, waylaying and killing them with the most savage barbarities.

It will not be amiss to observe here that the Pequot embassy to the Narragansetts was defeated of its purpose through the active and self-sacrificing labors of Roger Williams : his influence with the Narragansetts, among whom he lived and with whom he had established relations of friendship and confidence, being sufficient to restrain them from following Sassacus. In a letter to Capt. Mason he says : "Three days and nights my business forced me to lodge and mix with the bloody Pequot ambassadors, whose hands and arms methought recked with the blood of my own countrymen, murdered and massacred by them on Connecticut River, and from whom I could not but nightly look for their bloody knives at my own throat also." Bancroft gives Roger Williams the credit for "dissolving the conspiracy" against the whites. He adds: "It was the most intrepid achievement in the war, as perilous in its execution as it was fortunate in its issue." So the man whom the Massachusetts colonists had sent into exile was able to save them from the extermination which had surely been their fate had the Pequot-Narragansett alliance been formed.

Some thirty persons belonging to the settlements on Connecticut River having fallen victims to Indian barbarity, and it being manifest that the Pequots had entered upon a war of extermination, the Connecticut colonists were confronted with the problem, in its most practical and concrete form, of the survival of the fittest. This situation explains the subsequent action of Capt. Mason. What followed that action amply justified it.

The Pequot war was the first emergency the General Court of Connecticut was called to meet. The aid of the Massachusetts and Plymouth colonies, which had "raised the wasps," naturally was solicited. Massachusetts, at a special session of its General Court, responded with an order for a levy of one hundred and sixty men and the sum of £600. Plymouth ordered a levy of forty men. Connecticut raised a force of ninety men, forty-two of whom were from Hartford, thirty from Windsor and eighteen from Wethersfield, and placed them under command of Capt. Mason.

The formal declaration of war by the General Court of Connecticut was on May 1. On May 10, Mason, having completed the levy, started with his expedition down the river, the intention being to carry out the declaration literally by making an "offensive war" against the Pequots. Hence they were to be attacked in their stronghold here.

On the seventeenth of May, they arrived at Saybrook, where they remained wind-bound until the nineteenth. Saybrook was then simply a fortification with a small garrison under command of Capt. Lion Gardiner. which had lately been re-enforced by Capt. Underhill with nineteen men from Massachusetts.

Mason's army of ninety men was considered so absurdly inadequate to the task set before it that the trained soldiers, Gardiner and Underhill, at first refused to send any of their own men upon the expedition. Finally. Underhill with twenty of the garrison joined Mason. and twenty of Mason's original ninety were sent back for the protection of their own homes and families.

At this point a question arose upon the decision of which, as afterwards clearly appeared. the fate of the whole movement depended. It was in its essence a question of obeying instructions. Not only were they limited by the terms of their commission to landing in Pequot River. but the order had been repeated by a letter of instructions sent to Saybrook. But Capt. Mason, having made up his mind upon information received after leaving Hartford that the Pequots were aware of this design and prepared to meet them. was disposed to take the responsibility of disregarding his instructions in this particular and disembarking at a point farther east. "Our council," says Mason, "all of them except the captain, were at a stand and could not judge it meet to sail to Narragansett," in the face of such positive and repeated instructions to land at Pequot River.

Capt. Mason was a profoundly religious man, but there was something like worldly wisdom in his piety when, as he says, "Apprehending an exceeding great hazard in so doing," he "earnestly desired Mr. Stone that he would commend our condition to the Lord that night to direct how and in what manner we should demean ourselves in that respect, he being our chaplain and lying aboard our pink, the captain on shore." It is safe to say that before taking himself ashore, as he no doubt did to avoid the suspicion of having unduly influenced the chaplain, he took good care that Mr. Stone should have such knowledge of the facts as to be able to lay them intelligently before the Lord. At any rate, the chaplain's prayer was answered in accordance with Capt. Mason's view of the situation, and very early the next morning, by unanimous agreement of the council, the expedition set sail for Narragansett.

The strength of Mason's character, his manly self-reliance, and his patient self-command, are finely illustrated by this episode. The habit of his mind from his training as a soldier in the Low Countries under that famous disciplinarian, Sir Thomas Fairfax, was that of strict subordination and unquestioning obedience : but here was an emergency which called for something more. He must take the risk himself of disobeying orders to save the cause, or, avoiding responsibility, put the cause in serious peril by meek obedience. He chose the former. He did it with no less modesty than firmness. In his history of the Pequot war written thirty years later, he seems more anxious that it should not be regarded as a precedent than to take any credit for it to himself. After relating the transactions just described, he quaintly says : "I declare this not to encourage any soldiers to act beyond their commission or contrary to it, for in so doing they run a double hazard. There was a great commander in Belgia who did the state great service in taking a city, but by going beyond his commission lost his life. His name was Grubbendunk."

Leaving Saybrook on Friday, the nineteenth, they reached their destination in the evening of Saturday, the twentieth. The next day being Sunday, they remained on board their vessels, religiously keeping the Sabbath. A storm coming up prevented their landing until the evening of Tuesday, at which time they disembarked at the foot of what is now called Tower Hill, overlooking Point Judith.

On Wednesday morning. Capt. Mason called upon Canonicus, the chief sachem of the Narragansetts, with whom peace had been firmly established through the diplomacy of Roger Williams, and in courtly phrase explaining his sudden intrusion asked permission to pass through the Narragansett country on his way to punish the enemies of the Narragansetts, the Pequots. Canonicus answered, giving the desired permission and approving the design, but adding that their numbers "were too weak to deal with the enemy, who were very great captains and men skilful in war."

Here Mason received a message from Roger Williams, announcing the arrival at Providence of a Massachusetts party of forty men under Capt. Patrick, and requesting him to wait until they came up. But, with Mason, celerity of movement whereby he could take the enemy by surprise was of more importance than reinforcements. It is not an improbable inference from what subsequently happened, that Capt. Mason knew something about Patrick and preferred going on without him. It seems "there fell out a great contest" between Patrick and Underhill shortly after the two parties united at the mouth of the Pequot. A few years later, this same Capt. Patrick, having quarrelled with the Massachusetts people, went over to the Dutch at New Amsterdam and put himself under their protection.

Early Wednesday morning, Mason, with his seventy-seven white men — thirteen having been left in charge of the boats — about sixty Mohegans, and two hundred or more Narragansetts, took up his march against the Pequots. At the end of the day's march they came to a fort occupied by the Niantics, a tribe of the Narragansetts, it being on the frontier of the Pequots. These Indians showed at first an unfriendly disposition. Mason says, "They carried very proudly towards us; not permitting any of us to come into their fort." The Captain accordingly set a strong guard around the fort and ordered that no one should pass out during the night; a prudent precaution against the possibility of information being conveyed to the Pequots. Mason had no confidence in

Indian good faith; he distrusted these Niantics, notwithstanding they were at war with the Pequots against whom he was marching. To him the Indian was a very squalid and repulsive creature externally, with a treacherous disposition in which cowardice and blood-thirstiness were equally mixed; a very different figure from that which excites our admiration in the sculptor's marble or on the painter's canvas, or that attracts our sympathy in the pages of romance. He saw him in the concrete: a stealthy wild beast lurking in thickets, with but one ambition higher than slaughter, and that to torture his victim with refinements of cruelty before killing him. The early Puritan was somewhat deficient in artistic sense. It probably never occurred to John Mason, seeing this untutored child of nature with drawn bow or raised tomahawk, that the pose was dramatic. The first swift suggestion was that a funeral was impending, and his chief and immediate care was that it should not be his own.

Capt. Lion Gardiner, in command at Saybrook, had even less confidence in Indian professions than Mason. He would not trust the Mohegans—sixty of whom with Uncas had come to Saybrook by land from Hartford to join the expedition against their enemies the Pequots—until a party of them, sent out against a straggling band of Pequots, returned with one prisoner and the heads of five others. Chaplain Stone also distrusted the Indians. Capt. Underhill relates that going on board the chaplain's vessel, he heard him wrestling in prayer with the Lord that some sign of the good faith of the Mohegans might be given before they were taken on board. When he rose from his knees, Underhill told him his prayer was already answered, giving him the news of the return of the Mohegans with their bloody trophies.

But Mason, who was a discriminating judge of character, as well of the Indians as of his own countrymen, reposed much confidence in Uncas. So when on the next morning some two hundred of the

Niantics joined the little army, making about five hundred Indians in all, while they were boasting how brave they were and how many Pequots they would kill, he quietly asked the Mohegan chief what he thought the Indians would do. Uncas answered that the Narragansetts would all leave, but that he himself would never desert the English. "And so it proved," says Mason; "for which expressions," he continues, "and some other speeches of his, I shall never forget him. Indeed, he was a great friend and did great service."

It may be mentioned in passing that Mason's friendship for Uncas continued unbroken till his death in 1672. Uncas survived him ten years, and with his tribe was always a loyal friend and faithful ally of the whites.

At eight o'clock Thursday morning, Mason and his seventy-seven white men, with their noisy and demonstrative escort of five hundred savages, were on the march. The weather, it being the fifth of June in our calendar, was very hot and oppressive; there was a lack of provisions, and some of Mason's men fainted by the way. A march of twelve miles brought them to the Pawcatuck River, where they "stayed some small time," Mason says, and "refreshed themselves with their mean commons." Being now on the borders of the Pequot country, the boastful Narragansetts began to change their tune, "manifesting great fear," says Mason, "insomuch that many of them returned, although they had frequently despised us, saying that we durst not look upon a Pequot, but themselves would perform great things."

Three miles beyond the Pawcatuck, they halted at a field lately planted and held a council. Here they learned that the Pequots had two forts "almost impregnable," but, says Mason, "we were not at all discouraged but rather animated, insomuch that we were resolved to assault both their forts at once." One of them, in which was Sassacus the Pequot chief, was so remote that they could not reach it before midnight, so they were " constrained to accept of the nearest," being " much grieved thereat."

Encamping that night at Porter's Rocks " between the hills," they established their outposts, and with the rocks for pillows rested themselves after their weary march. Meantime the Pequots in their fort were keeping up a great rejoicing until midnight, the noise of which was heard by the sentinels. They had seen the expedition pass the mouth of their river some days before, and supposed that the English had not dared attack them. Hence their exultation.

Two hours before dawn they arose, joined in prayer, and began again their silent march, the Indians keeping so far in the rear that, upon reaching the foot of the hill, Mason sent for some of them to come up to act as guides. Only Uncas and the Niantic sachem Wequash appeared, who being asked where the rest were, answered, " Behind, exceedingly afraid." Whereat Mason sent word to them, " That they should by no means fly, but stand at what distance they pleased and see whether Englishmen would now fight or not "; a message imbued with the spirit, and almost in the language of Hebrew prophecy ; as when Jahaziel said to the affrighted hosts of Jehoshaphat, "Ye shall not need to fight in this battle ; set yourselves, stand ye still and see the salvation of the Lord."

The fort, though a rude defensive work, was quite formidable ; especially so considering the disparity in numbers between its seven hundred defenders and the seventy-seven assailants. It was circular in form, of an acre or two in extent, enclosed by trunks of trees driven into the ground, some ten or twelve feet in height. It contained about seventy wigwams along two streets or lanes, and had two openings at opposite sides for entrance and egress, which were closed by obstructions of light branches of trees.

The surprise was complete. The assault was made simultaneously at both entrances, Mason at one and Underhill at the other, with about sixteen men each, the remainder being ranged around the enclosure to prevent escape, and the Indian allies at a considerable distance where they had a safe point of observation and could without danger intercept fugitives with their arrows, which they did without mercy.

Capt. Mason on the northeast side was within a rod of the main entrance when the barking of a dog in the enclosure gave the alarm. Pushing his way through the opening, he found the camp in confusion, some of the Indians hiding themselves in their wigwams, others running about and hastily assembling themselves for resistance. There was some firing of muskets on one side and shooting of arrows on the other, but without much being accomplished, until Mason, realizing that the only chance his dozen or two men had against their seven hundred foes was to take immediate advantage of the panic, said, " We must burn them," and seizing a fire brand from one of the wigwams put it into the mats with which they were covered. The wind being from the northeast, the fire spread rapidly and overran the whole enclosure. Underhill and his detachment, being to leeward, were driven out by the flames. Mason, as soon as the whole fort was seen to be on fire, withdrew also and joined the reserves who, at a little distance, surrounded the stockade. Many of the Pequots were burned in their wigwams ; many others, climbing the palisades to escape the fire, met death at the muskets of Mason's men or were brought down by the Indian allies in the rear of the lines.

Of the seven hundred Pequots, only seven were taken captive and seven escaped. It is not probable that any women or children were in the stockade. No mention is made of them in either Mason's or Underhill's story of the fight. The only occupants of the fort were Pequot warriors, who had gathered here to repel Mason if he should land at the mouth of the river as was expected. Their number had been increased the night before the fight by the addition of some one hundred and fifty from the stockade on Fort Hill, in plain sight from this point, a mile or two distant, where Sassacus himself was.

Clearly, this was a bloody day's work ; a day of fire and slaughter. It is not altogether pleasant to think of, though two hundred and fifty years have passed. At the best. war everywhere. in all its immediate aspects, is repulsive. War is waste. Its wisest economy is often prodigality. It stops not to count with exactness. nor measures to the line. but scatters with reckless profusion and rends its fabrics with tooth and claw. It is well to remember, too. that from the beginnings of history, all progress has been in the wake of war, and every forward step in our boasted Christian civilization has been in its bloody footprints. And this was war in its worst form : a war of extermination on the one side, of self preservation on the other. It was short, sharp, and decisive, — none ever more so. And this is the comforting feature of it. that bloody and terrible as it all was. it resulted in an enormous saving of human life, and the prevention of barbarities beside which what happened here would have seemed but tender mercies.

It is not strange, however, that long after the event. when the conditions and surroundings were almost forgotten, and civilization had begun to ameliorate in some measure the horrors of war, the conduct of the fight should be criticized and the humanity of Capt. Mason called in question. It did not occur to Mason's associates. or the General Court under whose orders he acted, that there was any occasion for criticism. Mason made no excuses or explanations. The enthusiasm with which he was received on his return was unstinted ; the General Court raised no " Committee on the Conduct of the War," but signified its approval thereof and its confidence in Mason by appointing him to the chief military command of the colony.

Roger Williams, who would surely have been heard from had there been any ground for criticism of the transaction on the score of inhumanity, afterwards spoke of Capt. Mason, with whom he was in controversy, as having been made by the Lord " a blessed instrument of peace to all New England."

Capt. Underhill in his narrative of the fight, in a quaint and characteristic way anticipates possible criticism : "It may be demanded," he says, " Why should you be so furious? (as some have said). Should not Christians have more mercy and compassion? But I would refer you to David's war. When a people is grown to such a height of blood and sin against God and man and all confederates in the action, then he hath no respect to persons but harrows and saws them and puts them to the sword and the most terriblest death that may be. Sometimes the Scripture declareth that women and children must perish with their parents. Sometimes the case alters, but we will not dispute it now. We had sufficient light from the Word of God for our proceedings." The devout spirit of the Puritan preferred lodging his defence upon Scriptural analogies and his own interpretation of them, to the more natural and unanswerable appeal to the first law of Nature.

It is not impossible that there are those living within sight of this consecrated summit whose narrow view is confined to the bloody details of the fight, excluding causes, conditions, and results, and whose unreasoning sympathies are wholly given to the savage horde who only received here the measure they meted out ; who can see nothing in this passage in our early history upon which we may dwell with grateful emotions ; nothing in the character of the chief actor in it to awaken our enthusiasm or tax our admiration.

Looking out upon what has resulted from that morning's work on this hill, they may, if urged to the confession, admit that the

deliverance it accomplished, the saving of the seeds of New-
England civilization from the hoofs of barbarism, has been of
some service to mankind. But they would qualify the admission
by insisting that there was unnecessary bloodshed. For not
knowing the precise line to which they were required to hew on
the one hand, and might safely stop on the other, they censure
Mason and his men. For all the beneficent results that flowed
from their action, they piously thank God who overrules all things
to his own glory and who maketh the wrath of man to praise him.
It is our function here, while reverently acknowledging the over-
ruling Providence in history to consider also with reverence and
gratitude the instruments and methods by which it works. And
we are here, too. amid these peaceful scenes whose peace was
bought at such a price, to remember. first of all, that homely
axiom of common life. that " to have an omelet there must be
breaking of eggs."

Was it necessary to meet barbarians with barbarity, to apply the
burning brand that consigned these seven hundred to destruction?
Could not the end have been accomplished at a less sacrifice? Ask
Pastor Hooker, who at Hartford a fortnight before by a formal
religious ceremony had solemnly delivered the staff into Mason's
hands as the ensign of martial power, entrusting to his protection
the lives of the colonists. Ask Teacher Stone, chaplain of the
expedition, whose character and life assure us, even if his calling
had not forbidden it, that he would not approve unnecessary bloodshed. Ask the affrighted settlers at Wethersfield, whose husbands
and brothers had been tortured and slain, and whose daughters
had been carried into captivity worse than death. Ask Lion
Gardiner, who from his little fort at Saybrook had seen his men
ambushed and put to death with horrible torture. Ask the peace-
loving Roger Williams, who afterwards hailed Mason as " a blessed
instrument of peace to all New England." Finally, ask John

Mason himself, standing in the midst of overwhelming odds, within the very touch of their tomahawks, every wigwam bristling with arrows, and only restrained by momentary panic from bursting forth in a stream of red death upon him and his companions. Arrest his hand raised with the burning brand—ask him " cannot this sacrifice be avoided?" He need not speak. The scene itself, the conditions and surroundings, above all the first great law of nature, make instant answer.

Does your justification still lag, my peace-preaching brother? Lift up your eyes upon the scene spread out before you; upon these grassy hillsides sloping to the river and the sea, upon field and meadow waving with ripening harvests, upon farm and cottage, the rewards of toil and thrift, upon towns and villages teeming with life and humming with industry, upon yonder waters white with a commerce that keeps the world's remotest shores in constant touch. Slowly broaden your view till the tired eye of your fancy rests upon the Pacific shores ; gather in the vast intervening spaces reclaimed from savagery and waste for the occupation of sixty million people; turn the pages of history; note the growth and development of the nation, its beneficent influence in the march of human progress, its grand leadership in all that makes for the welfare of the world, in all that elevates and enobles man. All this had not been, had John Mason been less prompt or less resolute. Justified by all the existing conditions that influenced his action, he has been abundantly vindicated by the process of time, the award of history, and the judgment of posterity.

The practical annihilation of the Pequot garrison assembled here was not by any means the end of the perils by which Mason and his brave companions were surrounded. At the other Pequot camp on Fort Hill was Sassacus with several hundred warriors, now maddened to ferocity by the fate of their kindred. An attack from them in overwhelming numbers might be momentarily expected.

The Indian allies. with the exception of Uncas, had been found useless ; no help could be expected from them. In his history, Mason says : "And thereupon grew many difficulties. Our provisions and ammunition near spent : we in the enemy's country who did far exceed us in number, being much enraged ; all our Indians except Uncas deserting us ; our pinnaces at a great distance from us and when they would come we were uncertain. But as we were consulting what course to take it pleased God to discover our vessels to us before a fair gale of wind, sailing into Pequot harbor to our great rejoicing."

On their way to the boats. being encumbered with their wounded, twenty in number, they were set upon by Sassacus and some three hundred Pequots, through whom they painfully fought their way to the shore. Here they found their boats. which had been brought round from Narragansett Bay by Capt. Patrick of the Massachusetts contingent, who, for some reason, was not disposed to give Mason's men their own boats, whereupon a contention arose between him and Capt. Underhill. It was at length settled that the wounded should be taken in the boats, while Mason, with twenty of his men already weary with long marches and desperate fighting. should proceed on foot to Saybrook. They arrived there on Saturday night, the twenty-seventh of May (O. S.), June 7 in our calendar, and Mason says were " nobly entertained by Lieut. Gardiner and many great guns."

The Pequot war was practically ended. It had been formally declared by the Connecticut General Court on May 1 (O. S.). Within ten days Mason had raised his levy of ninety men. On the seventeenth he was at Saybrook, remaining there wind-bound two days ; on the twentieth he reached Narragansett Bay, kept the Sabbath next day on board, was prevented landing by the weather till the evening of the twenty-third ; was on the march through the twenty-fourth and twenty-fifth ; on the twenty-sixth destroyed.

the Pequot force on this hill, and on the twenty-seventh was at Saybrook, having marched the whole distance through an unbroken wilderness from Narragansett Bay to the Connecticut River. He had received no assistance from Massachusetts or Plymouth, and the Indian allies, except as guides, had been an incumbrance and hindrance. Massachusetts had "raised the wasps," Connecticut had burned them in their nest. The mischief kindled by John Endicott had been quenched by John Mason.

Since 1633, Massachusetts had been endeavoring to obtain satisfaction from the Pequots for the murder of Stone and his companions ; with the net result for the four years of fourteen Indians killed, a few wigwams burned, some canoes sunk, standing crops destroyed, and the Indians encouraged to active hostilities by the impotence of these demonstrations against them.

In April, 1637, the Pequots attacked Wethersfield. On May first Connecticut declared an offensive war. On the twenty-sixth she had finished it ; had made an end of the Pequot name and nation, saved New England, and established peace for forty years. If Connecticut has not been so forward as some sister commonwealths in raising wasps on this and other occasions, she has been behind none in the more difficult task of extinguishing them.

What followed is graphically described by Bancroft : "The vigor and courage displayed by the settlers on the Connecticut in this first Indian war in New England struck terror into the savages and secured a long period of peace. The infant was safe in its cradle, the laborer in the fields, the solitary traveller during the night watches in the forest ; the houses needed no bolts, the settlements no palisades."

Looking simply at the numbers engaged, the resources of military science displayed, and the duration of the action, the fight on this hill takes no rank in the annals of war. Pequot Hill does not appear in the list of historic battlefields, nor John Mason's name among the world's great captains. But it is not by the numbers engaged, the skill with which they are handled, or the stubbornness of the contest, that the importance of such a struggle and triumph as this can be rightly measured. The decisive battles of the world have been those on which the fate of races or the destiny of nations hung : the turning points of history. Such were the triumph of Arminius that broke the Roman yoke and created Germany, the rout of Attila at Chalons that arrested the Hunnish invasion and saved European civilization, the defeat of the Saracens by Charles Martel at Tours that turned back the march of Mahommedanism over Europe, the battle of Hastings which peopled with a new race the British Islands.

It is the decisive character of such events as these, as shown in their results, that gives them their highest importance. No less decisive and no less important in its consequences than any of them, or than the destruction of the Armada or the battle of Waterloo, was the speedy and effective work done by John Mason on this hill two hundred and fifty-two years ago.

A hundred years earlier, a similar tragedy had been enacted on a much more terrible scale when the soldiers of Cortez applied the torch to the temples which had become the last refuge of the Aztec people, and in the ashes of their capital extinguished the Aztec race. The triumph of the Spaniard meant for the conquered subjugation and slavery. The triumph of the English Puritan meant freedom and peace.

Upon the departure of Mason and his men, Sassacus and his followers, after some debate as to whether they should revenge themselves upon the Narragansetts or seek safety in flight, decided upon the latter and at once started westward to join the Mohawks west of the Hudson. Having killed some white settlers on their way, Mason with a force of one hundred and sixty men pursued and overtook about three hundred of them near Fairfield, where they had taken refuge in a swamp. Here they were surrounded, many of them killed or taken captive, only about seventy of them escaping, who made their way to the Mohawks. Sassacus was soon afterwards killed by the Mohawks, and the Pequot nation became extinct. In 1658, the name of the Pequot river was changed by the General Court to the Thames, and the settlement at its mouth to New London.

Returning to Hartford, Mason was appointed by the General Court the chief military officer of the colony, with the rank of major, which was equivalent to that of major general. This office he held for the remainder of his life, thirty-five years. When the fort at the mouth of the Connecticut was transferred to the jurisdiction of the colony, Mason was placed in command, and removing there became one of the first settlers of Saybrook. In 1659, he led in the first settlement of Norwich, where he resided until his death in 1672. During this time he held a great number of public offices of the first importance. In her " History of Norwich," Miss Caulkins distributes his life on this continent in four portions. He was " Lieutenant and Captain at Dorchester five and a half years, Conqueror of the Pequots, Magistrate and Major at Windsor twelve, Captain of the fort and Commander of the United Colonies at Saybrook twelve, Deputy Governor and Assistant at Norwich twelve." He died at Norwich, Jan. 30, 1672.

To the story of Mason's life and public services, distinct as it is in outline though scanty in detail, few words are needed in characterization of the man. It is in that quality or combination of qualities that we call balance of mind, a certain intellectual equipoise, that he excels all his contemporaries. A trained soldier, his whole life, with the exception of the brief intervals in which he was engaged in his sharp and decisive encounters with the Indians, was devoted to the pursuits of peace. The thirty-five years in which he held the chief military command of the colony were years of peace. A Puritan of the Puritans, he was no bigot. In the din of ecclesiastical controversies with which the colonies were filled, his only word was " that we look up to God to help us to see our evil and great folly in our needless strife and contention." A rigid disciplinarian, he did not hesitate to disobey the orders of the General Court in an emergency, in spite of the fate of Grubbendunk. Resolute and undaunted in danger, he was yielding and conciliatory when the danger had passed. With an indomitable will that surmounted all obstacles, and courage that could inspire his seventy followers to march against seven hundred, he combined that rare modesty and self forgetfulness of which later periods furnished such shining examples in Washington and Grant.

There is no manlier or more heroic figure than this in all our Colonial history. As pioneer, soldier, statesman, we cannot too greatly honor his memory. So, here, to-day, on the spot where, in the crisis of New England's fate, his unshrinking courage and decisive action determined the destiny of an unborn nation, we raise the figure that perpetuates in lasting bronze the deliverer of New England. But could the dead eyes be endowed with life, and the mute lips clothed with language, looking out upon the peopled continent and reading that wider tribute to his fame, he might well say : Let this be my monument ! *Exegi monumentum ære perennius.*

———

At the conclusion of the oration, Mr. Dyer introduced the poet of the occasion. Thomas S. Collier. of New London.

POEM.

Out from the dust and the ashes.
  Wherein we bury our dead.
Often an echo crashes.
  Like the call by a trumpet sped :
And deeds that were like the breaking
  Of seas on a rock-bound shore,
Rush in on the spirit. waking
  An ardor unknown before.
We feel that the past has spoken ;
  That the men who were mighty here.
Though they lie in a sleep unbroken.
  Have answered our triumph cheer.

Here, where the wild flowers cluster.
  And cool from the sweet salt seas.
The winds of the south-land muster.
  And harvest the song of bees,
Once there were blows. and the stinging
  Of bullets, whose whistle keen
The anthem of death was singing
  Through leaves that were fresh and green :

And high through the night's dark spaces
    The clamor of battle rose,
And the flames shone bright on the faces
    Of men who were bitter foes.

The years, like a fierce flood, wielding
    A power that no hand can stay,
Sweep on with a force unyielding,
    Till the past is swept away ;
But men who have shared the privation
    That has founded a nation's fame,
And given their blood as libation,
    Leave behind them more than a name.
They build for the future, unknowing
    Where the field of triumph lies,
And the graves that finish the showing
    Of their lives, seem a sacrifice ;
But the world with purpose is pregnant,
    Each day has its work and needs,
And acts, not names, are the regnant
    Role that the future reads.

Who knows of the men who slumber
    Because of the fight here won?
How great or how small the number?
    What deeds of valor were done?
Yet on through the forest, lying
    Like a snare before their feet,
With the wind in the new leaves sighing,
    They marched their foes to meet ;
Marched on where no foot before them
    Save the bear's or the wolf's had trod,

With the purple deeps high o'er them,
    And anemone stars in the sod,
These men who had left the beauty
    And light of a love-lit home,
And died at the shrine of duty,
    That peace with the years might come :
They built with their lives the glory
    And freedom wherein we share ;
It is ours to emblazon the story,
    And to keep their high fame fair.

Who were the men that we honor?
    Knights, with their lances at rest?
Princes, by Fame sought, to don her
    Chaplets of bravest and best?
Warriors, whose plumes led the battle,
    When from the flame-crested wall
Loud was the musketry's rattle,
    Louder the cannon made call?

No ; they were only the toiling
    Sons of the shop and the field,
Men on whose hands was the soiling
    Privation and labor will yield ;
Yet when the call for this sounded,
    Knights, aye, and princes were they,
Holding a faith strongly founded,
    Ready for ambush or fray.
On through the wilderness, lying
    Where the forest kings rose high,
And the shadows thrilled with the sighing
    Of echoes that whispered by,

They trod with a stern precision,
  As though the triumph was sure,
And they saw, as one sees in a vision,
  That they should increase, and endure.

The years have their seed and fruition.
  Men who are rulers of time,
Strong for each day's high mission,
  Fused in a mould sublime ;
Not theirs to stand idly waiting,
  Far from the fields of strife,
Even though scorn and hating
  Surge round each troubled life :
For like the far stars o'er us,
  Moving through cycles vast,
With the grand and resonant chorus,
  They sang in the mighty past.
Deeds that mankind must be doing,
  Come with the years that fly,
Always their end pursuing,
  Even though myriads die :
Man is the sword of the Maker,
  He who is ruler of man,
He is the moulder, or breaker,
  He is boundless and we are a span.

The rocks and the hills never perish,
  For they are the work of the Lord,
And so are the deeds that men cherish,
  Strong marks of the plough or the sword :
Each century keeps in its holding
  A purpose that cannot be stayed.

And days. months. and years are unfolding
  A record the ages have made.

Give them honor and praise and rejoicing.
  These men who were steadfast and strong ;
The wide land their courage is voicing.
  From orchards now ringing with song :
From factories filled with the clamor
  Of engines and looms never still ;
From shops where the loud-sounding hammer
  With the red mass of ore works its will ;
From shores where the white sails are gleaming ;
  From marts where the world comes to trade ;
From broad streams with rich commerce teeming ;
  From plain, mountain, hillside, and glade ;
From homes where love reigns with the olden
  Enchantment of beauty and trust ;
From farms where the wheat-fields are golden,
  And only the sword gathers rust :
They sleep. but the nation is keeping
  Their fame as a record and sign ;
They sowed what our hands now are reaping,
  The harvests of honey and wine ;
And never the meed of their labor
  In swift years shall lack fame or increase.
For they wrought with the musket and sabre
  The glory and gladness of peace.

The Rev. G. H. Miner, of Mystic River, then delivered the benediction, after which Colt's Band played a patriotic selection.

The procession then re-formed, the Governor and his staff reviewing the same, and the line of march for the return was taken up, the militia being dismissed at the central part of the village, where a collation had been arranged for them in a large hall. The Governor and his staff, and the other guests of the Commission, partook of a dinner at the Hoxie House, and at five the visitors took their trains for home, and the memorial was complete.

APPENDIX.

— ———

The Connecticut Historical Society,

Hartford, Conn., June 24, 1889.

Dear Sir, — My delay in acknowledging the invitation from your honorable committee to be present at the unveiling of Mason's monument is certainly not due to a lack of appreciation of the compliment nor to a failure to understand in a measure the high significance, of the event. I had hoped to be present at the exercises from the time when, a year ago, our society visited the site of the Pequot fort and Mason's camp at Porter's Rocks. But I am obliged reluctantly to give it up, as I must be here that day.

To me there is no more interesting or picturesque deed in all Connecticut history than Mason's expedition, if I except the meeting of Washington, Trumbull, Lafayette, Count Rochambeau, and others on the spot where I am now writing, which meeting resulted in the Yorktown campaign and the overthrow of British power. It always stirs me deeply when I think of that May morning in '37: the little army of 90 men bidding good-bye to wives, mothers, and sisters down on our " Dutch Point " ; or, gathered perhaps in the " Meeting-house Yard " or in the " Little

Meadow," listening while Thomas Hooker exalted their spirits, blessed their bodies, and exhorted their souls. What a mountain of faith must have been in the prayers of that company, when the three tiny ships slipped away from the improvised wharf and sailed down the Connecticut, bearing away to what must have seemed a veritable "Land of Divels" brave Mason, "New England's radient Crowne," Pastor Stone, and a large portion of the men of the little colony, including, may I add, one or more of my mother's ancestors in the company. It was almost sublime in daring, heroic in achievement. . . . . .

The state does well to build memorials to Hooker, and Davenport, and Mason. She adds to her dignity, and increases her honor and respect in the family of states by taking an active part in such celebrations as this, and the adoption of her, and the world's, first written constitution. The money is well spent, and will bear fruit in an object lesson not lost on us, youngsters and men of a later but, thank God! quieter day.

I trust our society will be represented by one or more of its officers, on Wednesday. With regrets that I cannot be there, I have the honor to be,

Your obedient servant,

FRANK B. GAY,
Secretary and Librarian Conn. Hist. Society.

AUBURNDALE, MASS., June 25, 1889.

GENTLEMEN, — Your invitation to the librarian of the New-England Historic Genealogical Society to attend the unveiling of Capt. Mason's statue comes tardily to my hands as chairman of its Library Committee. Our library just now has no librarian. We should be glad to be represented on so interesting an occasion, but it is not possible. Please be sure, however, that our interest in your work and its successful completion is most hearty. Connecticut honors herself and New England in such a memorial, as she has done in her recent Putnam monument. It is to be hoped that other states will emulate so good an example.

Yours very truly,

HENRY M. HAZEN.

CABINET OF THE RHODE-ISLAND HISTORICAL SOCIETY,

PROVIDENCE, R.I., June 19, 1889.

Messrs. C. A. Williams, Charles E. Dyer, and Richard A. Wheeler, Commissioners, etc.:

GENTLEMEN, — I thank you for an invitation to attend the ceremonies at the unveiling of the statue in honor of Capt. John Mason and his comrades on Pequot Hill, Mystic, Conn., the 26th instant, and regret that a previous engagement at Cambridge, Mass., will prevent my participating in the pleasures of that most interesting occasion. This society would, if it could, extend its cordial salutations to the citizens of Connecticut who have by this movement made an enduring record of heroic action for the cause of civilization and humanity.

Very respectfully,

AMOS PERRY, *Secretary and Librarian.*

PILGRIM HALL, PLYMOUTH, June 19, 1889.

GENTLEMEN, — A few days ago I received, as librarian of the Pilgrim Society, your invitation to be present at the unveiling of the statue erected to the memory of Gen. John Mason, the hero of the war with the Pequots, or as our Pilgrim Gov. Bradford styled them, the Pequents. It will doubtless be an interesting occasion, and although I shall not be able to be present, yet I thank you for the invitation. In our early colonial records I find the following, which may be of interest to you : —

"1637. At the Gen'all Court of o^r Sou^{r}aigne Lord, the Kinge, holden at New Plymouth the vijth Day of June, in the xiijth Yeare of the Raigne of our Sou^{r}aigne Lord, Charles, by the Grace of God of England, Scotland, France, & Ireland, Kinge, Defender of the Fayth, &c. Before

WILLIAM BRADFORD, gent., Goūnor, Captaine MILES STANDISH.
EDWARD WINSLOW.   TIMOTHY HATHERLEY, and
THOMAS PRENCE,   JOHN JENNEY, gentlemen,
justice of the peace of o^r soūaigne lord the kinge, and assistante in the goūment.

"It is concluded and enacted by the Court, that the colony of New Plymouth shall send forth ayd to assist them of Massachusette Bay and Coñectacutt in their warrs against the Pequin Indians in reveng of the innocent blood of the English wch the s^d Pequins haue barbarously shed, and refuse to give satisfacçon for.

"It is also enacted by the Court, that there shallbe thirty psons sent for land service, and as many others as shalbe sufficient to mannage the barque.

"Lieftennant William Holmes is elected to goe leader of the said company.

"Mr. Thomas Prence is also elected by lott to be for the counsell of warr, and to goe forth wth them.''

Then follow the names of forty soldiers who willingly offered their services to go upon the said service, with three others who "*will goe if they be prest.*"

Again thanking you for the invitation.

I am, yours, etc..

THOMAS BRADFORD DREW.

To Messrs. Williams, Dyer, and Wheeler, Commissioners.

P.S. — I said that Gov. Bradford styled that tribe of Indians the Pequents. He does so in his history : but this Court record has still another name. — " Pequins."

NORWICH, CONN., June 15, 1889.

Messrs. C. A. Williams, Charles Dyer, and Richard A. Wheeler:

DEAR SIRS, — Your kind invitation requesting my attendance at the ceremonies to be held on Pequot Hill. Mystic. Conn., on Wednesday, the 26th instant, at the unveiling of the statue erected in memory of Capt. John Mason and his comrades, is received.

As a lineal descendant of early settlers in Plymouth Colony, whose names are honorably recorded in the early history of New England among those engaged in the wars waged by whites against the Indians in defense of their homes, their families, and their posterity ; with not a drop of any but Yankee blood coursing through my veins, I take a lively interest in any event commemorative of the valor of those men who, by their strength and manly courage, and with their own right hands, hewed out a home for us who have come after them, in which we may dwell in peace and security, with none to molest or make us afraid ; and particularly as the near friend of one, now gone from us, who took so active an interest in instituting the movement, and, while living, did so much towards accomplishing the object, the culmination of which is the event to be celebrated, do I feel especially honored by your invitation, which is gratefully acknowledged.

With these feelings, I shall endeavor to be present on the happy occasion, and participate in the ceremonies mentioned.

Very truly yours,

S. S. THRESHER.